IMAGES
of America

GUND

Rita Swedlin Raiffe stands in her Brooklyn, New York, backyard with her Molly Bunny in 1934. Molly was made by her father and uncles in their toy company.

IMAGES
of America

GUND

Bruce S. Raiffe and Alex Baron Raiffe

ARCADIA

Copyright © 2005 by Bruce S. Raiffe and Alex Baron Raiffe
ISBN 0-7385-3710-1

First published 2005

Published by Arcadia Publishing,
Charleston SC, Chicago IL, Portsmouth NH, San Francisco CA

Printed in Great Britain

Library of Congress Catalog Card Number: 2004112891

For all general information, contact Arcadia Publishing:
Telephone 843-853-2070
Fax 843-853-0044
E-mail sales@arcadiapublishing.com
For customer service and orders:
Toll-free 1-888-313-2665

Visit us on the Internet at www.arcadiapublishing.com

Visit Gund at www.Gund.com.

*To the thousands of people who have worked for Gund
over so many years and to those who have hugged
a Gund soft toy and know how wonderful it feels.*

Gund's first patented product (1912) was this ride-upon duck, which opened and closed its beak as the child waddled along on its back. Products like these first distinguished the company and its founder, Adolf Gund, as being a source of unique and innovative products.

CONTENTS

FOREWORD AND ACKNOWLEDGMENTS

During the days that Alex and I spent reviewing our company archives, preparing for this book to be published, I was overwhelmed with the thousands of documents, photographs, advertisements, products, patterns, letters, and records documenting the company's history. With Gund's 106-year history and a mother and grandfather who had squirrel-like tendencies to keep wonderful things tucked away, I was fortunate to have access to bountiful archives.

All the people involved in this company's history can be proud of their accomplishments. The reputation Gund enjoys as an industry leader is a product of the hard work and consistent dedication to the founding values of quality, integrity, and innovation. This is a reputation Gund has enjoyed for many decades.

Today, Gund is represented by thousands of people working in many countries. Its products are considered the finest in the world by millions of experts. Those experts range in age from 4 to 84, but their expression of joy when hugging a Gund teddy bear is a sure sign of our success.

—Bruce S. Raiffe

During the two summers I worked in the Gund archives, I developed an intimate knowledge of that one small room containing thousands of items of memorabilia. I became acquainted not only with this small space but also with the history of Gund and the history of my family. This journey afforded me the unique opportunity to know my family members—those living as well as those who died before my birth—through their actions and deeds.

I would like to thank several people whose help was indispensable in the writing of this book. First, my father, with whom I worked closely these past summers, kept me focused and dedicated to the task at hand. Without him, of course, there would be no book. Second, I thank my grandparents Herbert and Rita Raiffe, collectors of the company archives who always provided clarification and explanation when I needed it. Third, I am grateful to my great-aunt Ceil Berman, whose reflections on her husband, John Swedlin, narrowed my research and provided insight into events in the company's history. Lastly, I thank Stacey Coleman, whose support and never-tiring patience kept me going and who picked up the loose ends when I began school again in September.

—Alex Baron Raiffe

INTRODUCTION

One can only imagine the excitement of Adolf Gund, who founded a new business in a new century and created some of America's first teddy bears! As a German immigrant, he resided in Connecticut and worked in New York City. His company was founded in 1898 as a novelty firm specializing in artificial flowers, beads, and gifts. But, in 1899, it began to make quality soft fabric animals.

In 1902, Pres. Theodore Roosevelt refused to shoot a baby bear while on a hunting trip in Tennessee. This event was politicized in a famous cartoon declaring the baby bear "Teddy's Bear." Ever since, stuffed toy bears have been named Teddy. Gund, however, had been making stuffed bears four years prior to the famous event. Today, Gund remains the country's oldest existing teddy bear manufacturer.

Adolf Gund's founding principles were quality and originality of design. He used the best textiles available and built a reputation that distinguished the company from its competition. Gund married but did not have any children. His company was later sold to a young man who demonstrated a good work ethic and a skill for toy design: Jacob Swedlin.

Jacob, a young immigrant of 12, asked Adolf Gund for employment in 1907. Working for Gund was his first job, and he took his responsibilities very seriously. Like many young men who had arrived in the new country, he felt an obligation to work hard and save money. He missed his parents and siblings still living in Russia and wanted to send them money so they too could immigrate to the United States. In this he was successful. Within 10 years, his entire family was living in New York City.

Continuing the company's traditions, Jacob Swedlin, along with brothers Abe and John, ran Gund for 40 years, starting in 1925. In this time, they built the company into a booming business, trading within the toy industry and acting as presidents of the toy industry association. Gund also enjoyed relationships with Hollywood studios, making children's animated films. The company pioneered the licensed product toy business.

The Gund manufacturing facilities were located in New York City—first in Manhattan and later in Brooklyn. In the early 1960s, John Swedlin visited Japan and developed relationships with several toy manufactures producing Disney products for the Japanese market. Thereafter, Gund started to import some of these products and sell them in America. These unique toys added to the company's ability to offer variety to its customers.

In 1956, Herbert Raiffe joined Gund after marrying Rita Swedlin, Jacob's daughter. Herbert's background as an accountant served him well, as his responsibilities related to production management and sourcing. His expertise enabled the expansion of Gund's manufacturing base in Japan, which later led to product sourcing in Taiwan, Korea, and China. In addition, Herbert opened production facilities for the company in Haiti and El Salvador. A perfectionist, he consistently worked on improvements to toy safety. Herbert became president of Gund in 1969; he is now retired and serves as chairman emeritus.

Rita Swedlin Raiffe joined Gund in 1972 with an interest in the artistic side of the company's products. Her design background enabled her to identify the need and create the solution to the industry's lack of "softness" in its soft toy products. Her under-stuffing techniques later became an industry standard, and her many collector designs are cherished by the teddy collectors in many countries.

Rita traveled extensively with Herbert to production and design facilities all over the world. Her input on the company's designs led to the growth in popularity of the Gund brand for the three decades she served as design director.

Bruce Raiffe began "working" for Gund when he was a child. Visiting the Brooklyn factory with his father and grandfather on Saturday mornings became a favorite event. Perhaps this is why, as a young boy, he dreamed of the day when it would be his turn to be president of his family's business. Joining Gund full-time in 1977 after a Wharton School education, Bruce served as salesperson, marketing director, and vice president before becoming president in 1993.

During Bruce's presidency, Gund's sales expanded threefold, and the company enjoyed growth in international markets. The strength of the company's BabyGund brand, "Gotta Getta Gund" slogan, and its relationships with well-known publishers and movie studios puts Gund at the top of its industry. The company also produces hundreds of custom-made products each year. These are used as premiums or by retailers that want to use a Gund item to promote their own business.

In July 2004, Bruce became the company's chairman, and Jim Madonna assumed the presidency. Jim has more than 25 years of industry experience and had been associated with Gund for eight years prior.

The company cherishes its rich history, the values of its founders, and the toys it has produced. The business principles of Adolf Gund served him well in 1898, just as they serve Gund 106 years later.

One

THE FOUNDING YEARS
1898–1925

After 12 years of business, on February 11, 1910, the company was incorporated in the state of New York. Its name was registered as "Gund Mfg. Co.," and it assumed the use of "GEE" as the first slogan used in its advertising and on its product labels.

Adolf Gund (1869–1945) was a distinguished American businessman of the early 20th century. He was born in Germany and resided in Norwalk, Connecticut, and New York City. In 1898, he founded a toy and novelty company that was incorporated under New York law on February 11, 1910, as the Gund Manufacturing Company.

Gund first produced its products in New York City loft factories. Pictured above are Gund's factory workers, early products, and Adolf Gund himself (first row, sixth from left) on the workshop floor. In 1899, the loft was located at 1315 Third Avenue. In 1904, it moved to 435 Broadway, to 22 West 19th Street, and then to 442 West 42nd Street. In 1922, Gund's factory and office were located at 25 East Ninth Street (shown above and below). As the company grew, it continuously needed larger manufacturing quarters. From those loft factories, Gund supplied its products to the growing toy industry.

A. GUND
~~RIDGEFIELD, CONN.~~
1938 Webster Ave
NEW YORK 57
N.Y.
Nov. 21ˢᵗ/43.

Dear Friends:

I am writing these lines to ask you to do me a great favor.

It seems these war years are good years for babies, where ever I go amongst my friends, there is one or two babies in the family or one on the way and as they all know Uncle Gund is a toy man, they expect me to furnish some toys. Therefore I want to ask, if you could possibly send me an assortment of about 10 toys, so I will be able to make those babies happy! Thank you.!!

I am feeling fairly well in spite of the load of years on my back getting heavier, but so far I, managed well to carry it and about the future — I do not worry.

With the summer gone and the nice fall days soon at an end, I have to look for inside work again to keep my mind busy, so if you should have use for an old toy man - think of me.

With Kindest regards to both of you and your families I remain with thanks
Sincerely your AGund

In 1943, several years before his death, Adolf Gund wrote this correspondence to his successors at Gund. Referring to himself as "Uncle Gund, a toy man," he requests a few toys to make his friends' babies happy and asks the company that when they "have use for an old toy man—think of me."

November 23, 1943

Mr. A. Gund
1938 Webster Avenue
New York 57, N. Y.

Dear Mr. Gund:

We were more than pleased to receive your letter of the 21st and also
glad that you are well.

We had to laugh at your advice about the fact that war years are good
years for babies.   It is unfortunate that babies cannot go to work
because we sure could use workers, particularly girls at machines and
boys in the Shipping Department.

As per your request, we are sending you a dozen assorted toys, which
you can distribute to your friends.   This certainly has been a
really tough year and very frankly, we are very happy that this year
is almost over.   Of course, no one knows what next year will hold
for us and maybe we should not be so glad that this one is over.
Next year may be worse.

However, we are more than thankful that in spite of difficulties, prob-
lems, etc, all of us have been spared the destruction and fighting
that is going on over there.

Please stay well.   We also hope that you will spend a pleasant
Thanksgiving Day.

Best and kindest regards from Jack and the writer.

                              Sincerely,

AS:MP   A. SWEDLIN

Abe Swedlin responded to Adolf Gund's 1943 letter warmly. Telling of the period, Abe notes
the difficulty in recruiting workers during the war years and gives thanks that America has been
spared the fighting and destruction going on in Europe. These letters demonstrate the warm and
friendly relationship shared by the founder and his successors.

Early Gund products are offered for sale in San Francisco, California. This Easter bunny display was presented to wholesale toy buyers at a trade exposition in 1928. Pictured with the merchandise is Eddie Barish, sales manager. Note the early Felix the Cat in the front row on the far left. Felix was first produced by Gund in 1921.

In 1922, a patent was received on Adolf Gund's creation of a springing dog. This product contained a mechanism that brought the stuffed toy "to life." Mechanisms not unlike these are found in contemporary toy designs. At the time, though, this innovation helped Gund establish its place as a creator of unique products.

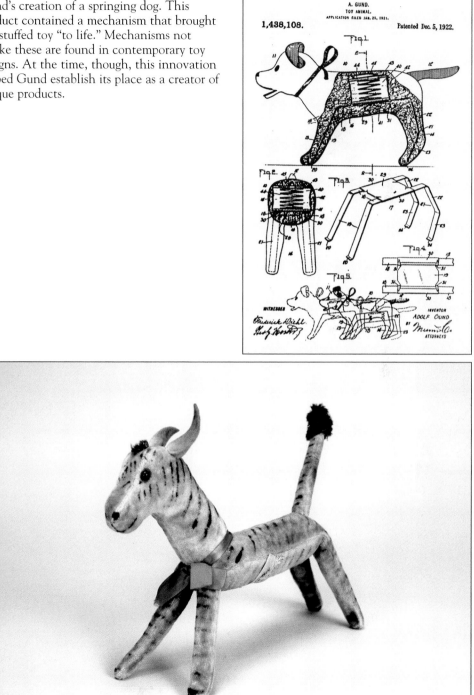

This printed velvet horse contains the mechanism described in the patent above. When the mechanism releases, the horse jumps a foot into the air.

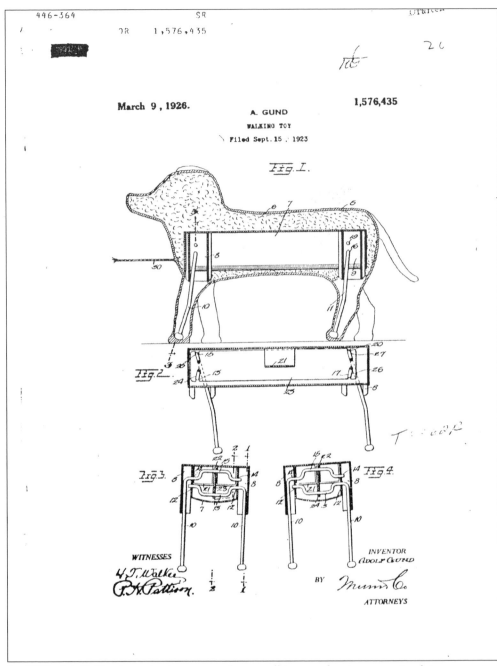

March 9, 1926.   1,576,435

A. GUND

WALKING TOY

Filed Sept. 15, 1923

Fig. I.

Fig.2.

Fig.3.   Fig.4.

WITNESSES
4.J.Walker
P.K.Pattison.

INVENTOR
ADOLF GUND

BY
Munn Co.

ATTORNEYS

In 1923, Adolf Gund received a patent for a walking mechanism contained in many toys produced by the company. At this time, stuffed toys often had mechanisms; Gund had been a leader in their design and production.

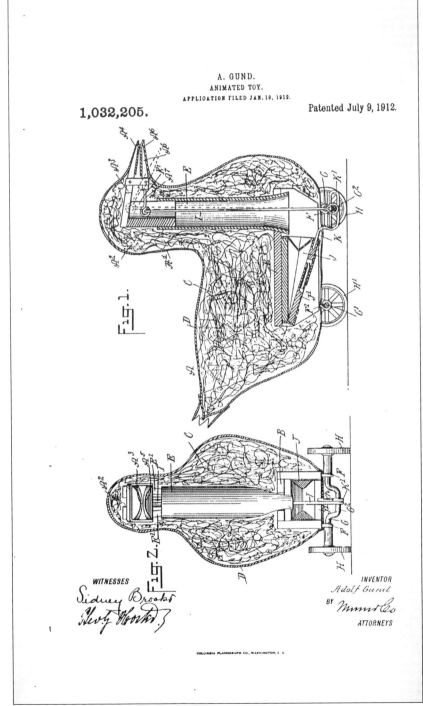

Adolf Gund received several U.S. patents for his unique creations. The earliest patent is for this mechanical ride-on duck. (See cover image.) The mechanism enclosed in the stuffed fabric body allows the duck's bill to move up and down as the wheels rotated with the child's steps. Patented in 1912, it was produced by Gund for 10 years.

GUND MANUFACTURING CO. of Norwalk, Conn.

PRESENT

"WA-GEE-WALKER"

ANIMALS

Protected by U. S. Patent

THEY WALK AND WAG

Greatest Achievement In Mechanical Toys

JUST TAKE THE ANIMAL BY ITS LEADER AND IT WILL FOLLOW YOU
WHEREVER YOU GO, and

WAG ITS TAIL AT THE SAME TIME

It is a simple, but most ingenious mechanism

Without the employment of Springs or any Sort of Clockwork, Nothing that Can Go Out of Order

We are offering now "WA-GEE-WALKER" Animals in the following styles and qualities:

PUPPY DOG & KITTEN, made of Velvet.
PUPPY DOG & KITTEN, made of Mohair Plush.
AIREDALE, made of Long Pile Mohair Plush.
WIRE HAIR FOX TERRIER, made of Long Pile Mohair Plush.

SAMPLES SUBMITTED ON REQUEST

YOU CANNOT AFFORD TO IGNORE THIS GREATEST OF ALL NOVELTIES FOR THE APPROACHING SEASON

"WA-GEE-WALKER" is his name
The greatest thing as Toy and Game.
I just need call him, without fail
He walks with me and wags his tail.

We will submit for samples or return them

This early trade advertisement features the 1923 patented mechanism (page 16) within a walking stuffed toy. The advertisement states, "It is a simple, but most ingenious mechanism." At this time, the company's products were made of velvet and mohair. These textiles are still used in some of the company's current products, as they represent some of the finest fabrics still available for manufacturing classic stuffed animals.

"Bunkie Dog"

Crying Cat

"Flip Flap Duck"
(Quacks and Flaps Wings when Moved)

GUND

Stuffed Animal
SPECIALTIES

Parrot, Cries when Moved

Duck, Quacks when Moved

THIS High Grade Line Comprises 200 Sure Selling Specialties in Velvet and Plush That Will Yield You Excellent Retail Profits.
Birds and Animals on Wheels That Cry When Pulled Over the Floor, Crying Animals and Birds, Bears, Dogs of All Kinds, Cats, Pigs, Monkeys, Elephants, Sheep, Goats, etc., etc.
The Quality Has Made Them Famous.

Place Orders Now for Prompt Deliveries

GUND MANUFACTURING CO.
220-230 West 19th Street, NEW YORK

Dog with Voice

Velvet Fox Terrier

Natural Wool Sheep

Squealing Pig

Stuffed Monkey

Kindly Mention PLAYTHINGS When Writing to Advertisers.

Playthings magazine was, is, and will continue to be the toy industry's leading trade journal. Gund chose to advertise in *Playthings* from the earliest publication. Advertisements from 1914 to 1927 show a variety of Gund's products. In this 1914 advertisement, the company features its line of 200 specialties that will yield "excellent retail profits." The descriptions reveal many wheeled products, as well as noise-making animals, especially unique at this time.

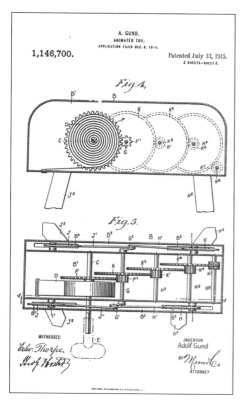

This patent, received in 1915, claims the invention of the wind-up walking mechanism used in many Gund products. The diagram to the left illustrates the spring and gears that powered the four legs. Once the device was placed inside a toy or doll, a key was used to wind the spring. The mechanism fit nicely within dolls and animals, as illustrated below.

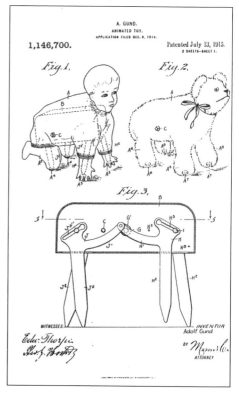

In 1915, the company claimed the demand for its line "has compelled us to seek newer and larger quarters," as it continued to introduce more mechanical toys and "High Grade Stuffed Animals." The January exhibition of toys at the Broadway Central Hotel was a predecessor to the International Toy Show, which still occurs in New York each February. The Broadway Central Hotel was located at 200 Fifth Avenue and later became the International Toy Center. This advertisement features the products containing the patent on the previous page.

This horse can walk by means of the wind-up mechanism shown in the 1915 patent. Made of a cotton material, it wears a wool felt blanket. The horse's facial features have been painted, and the bridle and mane are made of wool trimmings.

"GEE"   "GEE"
GUND MFG. CO.
CREATORS OF NOVELTIES
INTRODUCE
"PUPPY GRUMPY"
(COPYRIGHTED)

The Latest Hit in a Character Dog

So Lifelike that no one can help taking him Home "for the Kiddies." Made in White or Tan Velvet with Contrasting Colors for Ears and Tail. Colored Ribbon around Neck and

A Cute Puppylike Bark

Write for Samples Today—Deliveries in Rotation as Received

Retails $1.00 with Good Margin
OUR WELL KNOWN LINE OF
STUFFED ANIMALS

and Plush Novelties is Selling Bigger than Ever. We are Practically Sold Up for the Season but All Orders Received in Time Will Be Taken Care Of.

GUND MANUFACTURING CO.
34 UNION SQUARE   NEW YORK

In 1919, Gund introduced Puppy Grumpy (left) and rocking toys (below) to the trade. The advertisement below also notes the first Easter line the company offered. In 1919, Gund's products were well diversified between dolls, stuffed toys, mechanical toys, and seasonal gifts.

SOMETHING NEW AGAIN!
Gund Manufacturing Company
34 Union Square, NEW YORK

Well known originators of novelties, introduce herewith their latest mechanical creation:

"THE ROCKING TOYS"

Our Rocking Toys are very attractive, made in different characters as Doll, Cat, Bear and Dog, sitting in a neatly finished Rocking Chair, made of strong, bright colored wire; operated by clock work, the toy starts to rock and keeps on rocking for about two minutes, to the great amusement of young and old. They certainly will prove to be big sellers.

FULL LINE OF EASTER NOVELTIES
as Rabbits, Ducks, Chickens, etc., in different positions and large varieties of sizes and colors.

COMPLETE LINE OF STUFFED ANIMALS
Made of Best Quality Plushes and Velvets

Dogs, Cats, Bears, Elephants, Horses, Lions, Tigers, etc., in great variety of sizes and at attractive prices. Prices on our line have been figured as low as possible under existing conditions of labor and materials. Every item is up to the well-known standard. We lose no opportunity to improve our line.

SOMETHING NEW COMING! WATCH!!

Gund continued to sell its products under the GEE line of animals in its 1927 advertisement for popularly priced animals (right). In 1922, the company advertised the Duckie-Quack-Quack (below), featured on page 17.

In the 1920s, Gund created many animals of real fur. This dog is fashioned of angora to create a realistic effect. Note the tag and logo that represented the company during these early years.

This Gund monkey was another mechanical invention. The monkey's arms were wound in one direction; when the mechanism was released, the toy flipped over to delight the child.

The arm of the monkey shown on the previous page exhibits the GEE trademark and offers directions to the child playing with this tumbling toy.

In 1917, the company's trade advertisement featured the GEE trademark, as the Gund name became a famous brand among stuffed toy manufacturers. This advertisement sells the mechanical menagerie, which included more than 30 styles of stuffed toys containing mechanical devices. Each toy moved, jumped, walked, or sounded to entertain the child at play.

These two dancing toys, Felix the Cat and Bluebird, include a patented mechanism filed by Adolf Gund. When wound, the toys wiggled and wobbled.

MECHANICAL CHARACTERS

No. 5926

Dancing Duck. A quaint number done in velvet with wings of three contrasting colors. Stands 10½ inches.

This line of mechanical dancing animals is one of the BEST and most POPULAR ON THE MARKET TODAY. Every number is attractive, flashily dressed and WELL made. A feature display will sell a great many of these dancers. Attention is called to "Felix the Cat," that famous movie cartoon character. Each dancer packed in an individual, attractively lithographed box.

No. 2923

Dancing Felix the Cat. Pat Sullivan's famous movie character. Measures 10½". Dressed in Velvet. Has glass eyes, glass nose and felt ears.

No. 2928

Dancing Bluebird. A happy number backed in blue velvet and breasted in red velvet with tri-colored wings measuring 10½"

No. 2933

Dancing Bell Hop Monkey. Dressed in red imitation jacket, and black trousers, has buttons on breast and wears a red cap.

Featuring dancing toys, this advertisement shows Felix the Cat and Bluebird.

In 1921, Gund signed a contract authorizing the production of Felix the Cat under license of its creator, Pat Sullivan. The company enjoyed great business from this licensed character. Here, an early Felix is dressed as a policeman.

Two

BUILDING A BUSINESS
1925–1969

Gund developed and used these three logos on its business documents, products, and advertisements between 1940 and 1970. The logo with ears on the "G" was successful in helping to identify the company's playful products with its name.

Jacob Swedlin, a Russian immigrant, arrived in the United States in 1907. His first job, at age 12, was as a porter in Adolf Gund's toy factory in New York City. Recognizing the boy's industriousness, Adolf Gund taught "Jack" to become a cutter and pattern maker. When Gund retired in 1925, Jacob was able to purchase the company for $1,500. Jacob asked his brothers Abe, Mike, and John to join him in the company's management; together they continued the established tradition of producing quality toys. Gund prospered under their leadership for four decades.

Shown here in the mid-1950s are, from left to right, John, Abe, and Jacob Swedlin with one of Gund's large Easter bunnies. The brothers were hardworking, loyal, and proud of their accomplishments as immigrant businessmen. Community leaders, they spent time with one another in social and business affairs. Both Abe and John served as presidents of the Toy Manufacturers of America, a respected industry association.

**An Announcement of Removal
A Cordial Invitation and
Greetings for the New Year**

HIRTEEN was lucky but bigger things call for roomier quarters...so we've packed Roxy, Tabby and Felix and Fido and Bunny and trundled them to a newer and more beautiful home at

FORTY WEST TWENTIETH ST.

The honor of your presence is cordially invited whenever you're in the neighborhood to make Gund's Stuffed Toy Headquarters your own quarters, and incidentally, congratulate the Swedlins on their novel display of originalities.

If we could stuff all the good things of life into a new number and call it "1930" we'd present it to you with our best wishes.

GUND MANUFACTURING CO.

J. SWEDLIN, Inc., *Successors*

New Number
WATkins 0037

40 · W · 20

Extra Line
WATkins 0038

NEW YORK

The year 1930 began an era of growth for Gund. Under the capable leadership of the Swedlin brothers, Gund pursued business vigorously. Beginning with a move to a new manufacturing space on 20th Street in Manhattan, Gund advertised their success to the trade.

Standing in front of a Gund display in their New York factory are, from left to right, Abe, Jacob, and John Swedlin. Abe acted as the financial officer for the company. He met with the company's bankers and ran the accounting, billing, and employment office. Jacob designed, calculated costs, and oversaw production. John ran the sales force and promotions, including all trade shows. He was also the driving force establishing relations with movie and television studios for the company's licensed products.

The Swedlin brothers and friends pose with an early collection of Disney licensed products (a relationship that began in 1947) and several Gund toys and dolls. Pictured here are Gund's Honey Lou doll, Donald Duck, Mickey Mouse, and Gus. This photograph was taken at the company offices, located at 40 West 20th Street in Manhattan.

The sales team is seen in the company's showroom. From left to right are M. C. Sussman, John Swedlin, Leo Scherrer, and Sam Kaye. Note the Disney products on the table and the variety of Gund products available on the shelves, including Bongo and Lu Lu Belle and four-circle designs popular at the time.

GUND - MATS LIKE THESE... *CATCH THE EYE!*

MICKEY MOUSE

MINNIE MOUSE

PANDAGUND

CUBBIGUND

ZIPPER KITTIGUND

Your all-star cast of **WALT DISNEY CHARACTERS**, perfectly re-created by GUND, captured in sparkling ad-mats for your own promotion!

DUMBO

PLUTO

DONALD DUCK

The introduction of Disney characters in the 1940s and the development of Gund's basic lines enabled the sales force to supply all major toy retailers across the country. This page shows only a few of the many products offered for sale at that time.

Donald Duck, Daisy, and their nephews were captured in the Gund product lines in the mid-1940s. They were created of acrylic plush with felt-trimmed feet and facial features.

Gund was proud of its extensive relationship with the Walt Disney Company. Here, Pinocchio is created as a soft Gund toy.

Some products featured simple mechanisms combined with Gund's quality softness. This beautifully crafted dog sits upon a steel frame and wheels, allowing it to become a "pull-along toy."

Party Tendered to
The Gund Family.
Hotel Taft. N.Y. City. Mar. 7. 1945

Toy fairs each winter were always a time for celebration. This 1945 Toy Fair dinner party for the Gund team, held at the Taft Hotel in New York City, was no exception. The company struggled through the war years to keep its doors open and to supply the industry with its fine products for children. This year's celebration had a very special meaning.

In the seat of honor is John Swedlin at his bachelor party in May 1945. Given by his brothers, the dinner included many Gund sales executives all celebrating his marriage to Ceil Cohn. Standing at the head of the table are, from left to right, Jacob Swedlin, Samuel Kaye, John Swedlin, unidentified, Abe Swedlin, and Mike Swedlin.

TO · THE · FAMILY · OF

L. John Swedlin

WE, the officers, directors and members of the advisory committee of Toy Manufacturers of America, pledge ourselves to honor the memory of L. John Swedlin, former president of our organization and a good friend and valued associate. His outstanding record of service over many years to his fellow manufacturers will long remain an example worthy of emulation by those who take on the responsibilities of association leadership.

Lionel Weintraub   Edwin W. Nelson, Jr.   Arthur L. Stoecklin

Nathan Cooper   Walter W. Armatys

William H. Duerig	Fred Ertl, Jr.	Arnold Frank
Leonard E. Greenberg	James J. Shea, Jr.	Manuel M. Frome
W. C. Keyes	H. Ric Luhrs	Walter L. Ross
William R. McLain	Mrs. Min Horowitz	Jerome M. Fryer

Unfortunately, John Swedlin, the youngest brother, passed away on July 31, 1969. This proclamation by the Toy Manufacturers of America pledges to honor the memory of John, their former president (1964) and industry leader. John had begun his career at Gund in 1939.

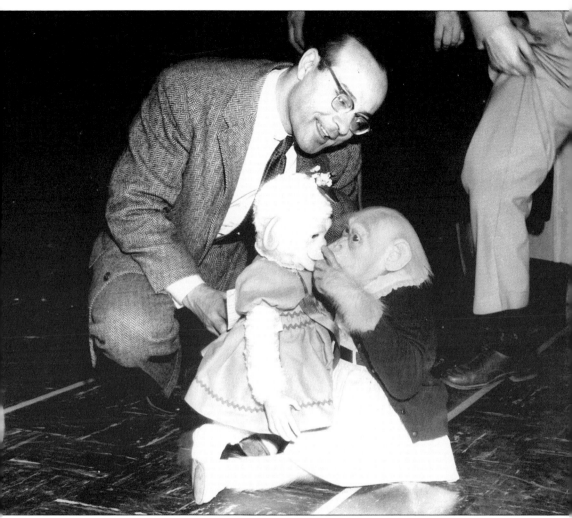

John Swedlin always wore a smile and had a wonderfully gregarious personality. No wonder he became the company's vice president of sales and led a successful team of salespeople. John later traveled to Asia, establishing relationships with Japanese suppliers. He succeeded Jacob as the company's president. Here, John is pictured with two white chimps: Zippy, produced by Gund, and one made by Mother Nature! Zippy was a television character of the early 1960s.

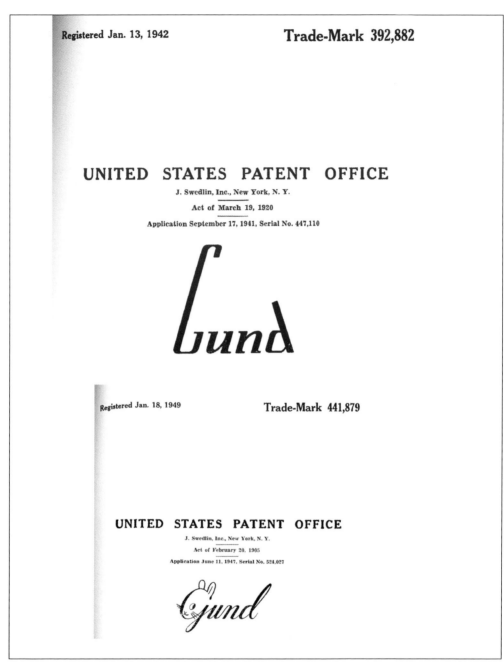

Registered Jan. 13, 1942　　　　　　Trade-Mark 392,882

UNITED STATES PATENT OFFICE

J. Swedlin, Inc., New York, N. Y.

Act of March 19, 1920

Application September 17, 1941, Serial No. 447,110

Gund

Registered Jan. 18, 1949　　　　　　Trade-Mark 441,879

UNITED STATES PATENT OFFICE

J. Swedlin, Inc., New York, N. Y.

Act of February 20, 1905

Application June 11, 1947, Serial No. 524,027

Gund

Gund received a federal trademark registration for the upper design of its name in 1942. The use of this trademark was limited, although the logo did appear on company documents and products for about seven years. The company received a federal trademark for the lower design in 1949. The animal ears and whiskers on the "G" represented the company for three decades and captured the fun spirit of its products.

The popularity of the Gund logo with a scripted "G" and bunny ears demanded a character. Therefore, Gundy was created. The first known sketch of the character is shown here. The name "Gundy" has been used many times on the company's products.

Gundy was created as an icon of the company. Shortly thereafter, the Gund Club was formed. All those who joined received a certificate like this one, from 1962.

The Easter promotion for 1936 boasts of real value and asks trade buyers to order early, as demand is ever increasing.

These Gund Easter products were popular in the mid-1930s. Dressed Easter bunnies were a company specialty, demonstrating the uniqueness that differentiated Gund's Easter products at that time.

Three women promote Gund's bunnies at a trade show *c.* 1930. Shows took place in various hotel ballrooms throughout the country. Wholesale buyers would place orders in the fall for spring holiday deliveries. The bunnies, made with rayon plush material and glass eyes, were filled with excelsior stuffing.

In 1928, Liggett's Drug Store in Grand Central Station, New York, displays Gund dogs in its window. The window features Gund's patented barking dogs, which contained a mechanical noisemaker within. Seated dogs not unlike these patterns continue to be sold by Gund today.

Another window display features Easter bunnies by Gund. Pharmacies and drugstores have been a strong part of Gund's retail network for more than 70 years. In this *c.* 1930 photograph, the shopkeeper understands the importance of "impulse" in attracting customers into the store to purchase bunnies. Gund was well known for its dressed Easter bunnies. All clothing on the bunnies was of unique fabric and had to be starched and pressed before the bunnies could be shipped to stores.

Inside Liggett's, the Easter display is attended by an appropriately dressed, festive sales attendant.

This additional photograph shows the inside display of Gund's Easter products at Liggett's Drug Store. Easter was, and still is, a major gift-giving holiday.

Liggett's in Grand Central Station, New York, displays Gund cats and dogs in a 1932 summer promotion. Displays like this are effective in creating an impulse desire to purchase Gund products. Similar displays continue to be used by many retail stores to enhance sales.

The 1931 Chicago Toy Fair shows a traveling display of Gund's line for purchase by wholesale buyers. This show took place at the Stevens Hotel. The company sent its road sales force to many events like this with various samples and displays. Gund became a national brand in the 1930s and 1940s because of the network of salespeople under the leadership of M. C. Sussman and John Swedlin.

Gund's puppy purse is modeled by a young Rosalie Swedlin, the daughter of John. This purse concept was originally introduced by Gund in the 1930s and was reintroduced in the early 1950s, when this photograph was taken. It emerged for a third time in the 2001 Gund line as a contemporary trend.

These are two of the many puppy purse designs sold by Gund in 2004.

In a c. 1930 letter to its customers, the company proposes a sample assortment of puppy purses for retail sale. The wholesale cost of $7.50 per dozen includes a Scottie, Airedale, terrier, and bulldog.

Gund Puppy purses were originally launched in the 1930s. This page boasts of the innovation and its sure popularity with young girls. Today, the company sells modern versions of these original creations.

Easter promotions are always successful. H. C. Prange, a Wisconsin department store and Gund customer, wrote a note of thanks to John Swedlin in 1948 for helping to make its Easter a great success. Seasonal products for Easter, Valentine's Day, and Christmas remain popular gifts for children.

Gund moved to its permanent showroom in the Chicago Merchandise Mart in 1937. This showroom served the increasing base of Midwest customers with full displays of the company's products (right). Maxwell C. Mechner was appointed to man the showroom (above).

Announcing a permanent
CHICAGO showroom
for

GUND

WE have had this in mind for some time. Chicago and the great Mid-west, which have patronized us so generously, certainly deserve the consideration . . . a new PERMANENT showroom in the famous Merchandise Mart, supervised by our Mr. M. E. Mechner, who will be on duty in Chicago when not actually traveling among our Western customers. Room 14-D2 will open about the first of December . . . and may all hands profit by the convenience of the new arrangement. Make yourselves at home!

EASTER Animals
We can't afford not to be ready for those who are already Easter-minded . . . so the new 1938 lines are "off the press" and waiting for your inspection.

Made in America by American labor

GUND MFG. CO., (J. Swedlin, Inc.; Succ.)

NEW YORK   CHICAGO   SEATTLE   LOS ANGELES   SAN FRANCISCO

In July 1938, Gund became one of the first tenants in the Fifth Avenue Building, located at 200 Fifth Avenue in New York City. This building, later known as the International Toy Center, still remains a toy industry headquarters and has been the home of the Toy Fair ever since. Gund continues to occupy the original second-floor rooms.

56

Abe Swedlin (seated, left front) joins in an August 1938 sales presentation at the company's showroom in New York City. This is likely one of the first business meetings in a showroom continuously used by the company for nearly 70 years.

"It must be good to be a Gund" is the early (1943) use of the stylized "G" to look like an animal head. This advertisement features the Dreamie line, which popularized Gund's lying down products. The eyes of these toys closed as they were laid down to sleep and opened again when picked up. The use of these "doll eyes" in a vinyl-faced plush toy was innovative at the time.

...to be a *Gund*....

You are Cordially Invited

to ROOM 232 at 200 FIFTH AVENUE

to see the **GUNDS** that make their

glamorous debut during the current Toy Fair

421/4 — Percale Cuddle Bear
Design Patent
Nos. 132,514 and 132,509

411/4 — Percale Cuddle Cat
Design Patent
Nos. 132,515 and 132,510

420/4 — Percale Cuddle Panda
Design Patent
Nos. 132,512 and 132,509

A MESSAGE TO REGULAR ACCOUNTS....
AND AN APOLOGY TO PROSPECTS

Our line for 1943 carries forward the Gund Tradition for quality of workmanship, originality of conception, and durability of construction. Despite difficulties in materials and labor, it is our intention never to deviate from our established high standards of craftsmanship . . . To the wave of inquiries from prospects, we must answer, with deep regret, that in fairness to our long-maintained connections we cannot now add names to our list of accounts.

The advertising copy also speaks of the company's regret in not opening new accounts. The war in Europe severely limited Gund's production capacities.

The Dreamie line of toys, including the pictured Dreamie Cat, was popularized by Gund in the early 1940s. This cat lies upon a box used to package all Gund products being shipped to stores. The box served to protect each toy in transit and could also be used for a gift. Used for 20 years, these colorful boxes became a part of the company's image to the consumer and the trade.

This sales flyer promotes the patented Dreamie Bunnies in 1942.

In 1938, Gund received an award for its use of a wonderfully designed gift box. For decades, all Gund products were shipped to stores in these attractive boxes.

These four-circle bears are typical of the bears Gund produced in the 1940s. The circles on the arms and legs gave the design its name and allowed for the use of contrasting fabrics.

As Ever, the F.F.G. [Famous Family of Gunds] Holds its Standards High...

As we advance into another year, we will hold steadfast to the line that "Gund means Genuine Value" and will carry forward the principles of quality, originality and craftsmanship maintained for more than two generations.

Conditions compel us to continue our quarter sales policy

GUND means real value in **STUFFED TOYS**

Gund MANUFACTURING COMPANY

NEW YORK · CHICAGO · SAN FRANCISCO · LOS ANGELES · SEATTLE

J. SWEDLIN, INC., *Successor*, 200 Fifth Ave., New York, N. Y.

During the war years, Gund creations were illustrated with uniforms, flags, and banners to show the company's support of American soldiers (left). FFG (Famous Family of Gunds) promoted genuine value while also speaking of "the present critical period of manufacturing difficulties" (below).

The F.F.G. Keeps its Banners High!

In the parade of outstanding playthings, the F. F. G. (Famous Family of Gunds) holds front-ranking position. . . . Through two generations this leadership has been earned by unfaltering adherence to the highest standards of quality, originality and craftsmanship. . . . Even through the present critical period of manufacturing difficulties there is no deviation from the principle that "*Gund means real value in Stuffed Toys.* . . ." Gund quality will remain enduringly — and so will the Gund reputation. . . .

> **Explanation to New Inquiries**
> Due to conditions it is necessary for us to confine our present distribution to our old regular customers. Therefore, we are compelled to defer adding new names to our list of accounts until such time as more normal trade circumstances prevail.

GUND means real value in **STUFFED TOYS**

Gund MANUFACTURING COMPANY

NEW YORK · CHICAGO · SAN FRANCISCO · SEATTLE

J. SWEDLIN, INC., *Successor*, 200 Fifth Ave., New York, N.

NO TOY FAIR

...but NO need for despair by "Gundealers"

Even though the Toy Fair has gone the way of most 1945 conventions the cloud is not without a silver lining for Gund customers . . . Some Gunds will be available, as smartly styled and quality-built as ever . . . We will do our utmost, within the confines of prevailing limitations, to provide our patrons with as many Gunds as conditions will permit. We ask them to be patient for just a short while.

GUND means real value in STUFFED TOYS

Gund

NEW YORK • CHICAGO • SAN FRANCISCO • LOS ANGELES • SEATTLE

MANUFACTURING COMPANY

J. SWEDLIN, INC., Successor, 200 Fifth Ave., New York, N. Y

Tell them you saw it in TOYS and NOVELTIES

In 1945, the Toy Fair was cancelled. The war in Europe and the Pacific had a severe impact on American businesses; the toy industry was no exception. Gund continued to support its customers with "as many Gunds as conditions will permit."

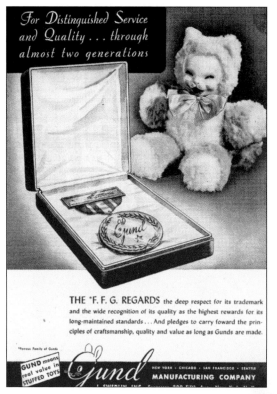

The four-circle cat (left) and bunny (below) each have a painted vinyl face and are made of rayon fabric. These designs typify the toys produced by Gund in the mid-1940s. In 1945, Gund advertised its desire to introduce many new products once peace is announced.

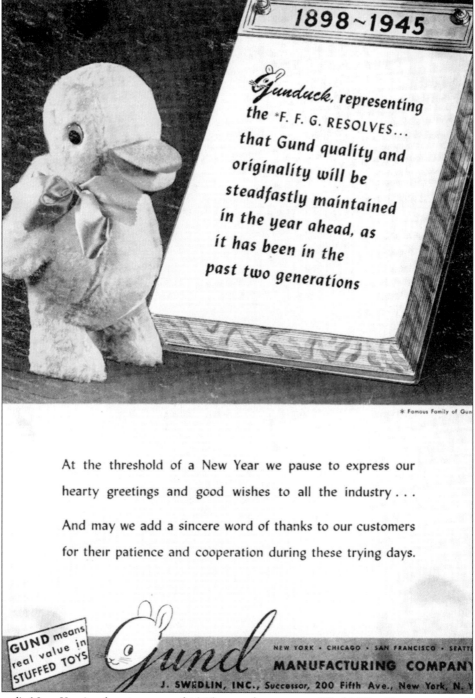

1898~1945

Gunduck, representing the *F. F. G. RESOLVES... that Gund quality and originality will be steadfastly maintained in the year ahead, as it has been in the past two generations

* Famous Family of Gun

At the threshold of a New Year we pause to express our hearty greetings and good wishes to all the industry . . .

And may we add a sincere word of thanks to our customers for their patience and cooperation during these trying days.

GUND means real value in STUFFED TOYS

Gund

NEW YORK · CHICAGO · SAN FRANCISCO · SEATTL

MANUFACTURING COMPANY

J. SWEDLIN, INC., Successor, 200 Fifth Ave., New York, N. Y

Gund's New Year's advertisement of 1945 prays for peace as World War II rages on. It also thanks customers for their "patience and cooperation during these trying days." Gund still offered its products, but on a quota allotment policy.

The F. F. G.* WELCOMES OUR BOYS HOME!

FROM GUNS TO GUNDS ... Many of the boys who

left our plant for the far-flung fronts will soon be returning to

us . . . And as they resume their various duties we shall, in

time, find opportunity to fulfill our post-war program of More

and Better Gunds . . . But it will be more than an over-night job.

So please be patient for just a little while longer . . .

*Famous Family of Gunds

GUND means real value in STUFFED TOYS

Gund

NEW YORK • CHICAGO • SAN FRANCISCO • LOS ANGELES • SEATTLE

MANUFACTURING COMPANY

Welcome home, soldiers! The company celebrates the end of the war and looks forward to resuming its postwar program of "more and better Gunds." All veterans who returned to Gund were welcomed at their old employer and gladly put back to work for the company.

During World War II, Gund created and sold this doll in an army uniform. Part of Gund's efforts to encourage the purchase of war bonds, it was also designed to support the morale of those at home during these most difficult years.

Finally, Good Schmoos tonight! Many major department and chain stores sold Good Schmoos to celebrate the good news in Europe. The Schmoos were a fad that lasted only two years. However, the fad was very significant to the industry and had a product life not unlike fad consumer products in soft toys today.

The year 1947 was Gund's 50th anniversary in business. Many trade advertisements were created to celebrate this accomplishment and, as seen below, to reestablish Gund's business in the postwar years. The advertisement to the right boasts of the company's fine reputation for quality and industry leadership.

Blue Ribbon Members of the "Famous Family of Gunds"

"We're **Good** because We're **Gunds**"

These Lammigunds are proud of their quality-heritage that dates back to 1898 . . . For almost half-a-century Gund crafts-men have applied the best of efforts and materials into mak-ing the finest stuffed toys their skill could provide. Their workmanship justifies the traditional slogan . . . "It's got to be good to be a Gund" . . .

See the new Gund line for Fall and the holidays. Each creation is a *Value* in *Quality* as well as in *Price*.

Since 1898 **GUND** means real value in STUFFED TOYS

Gund NEW YORK • CHICAGO • SAN FRANCISCO • LOS ANGELES • SEATTLE **MANUFACTURING COMPANY**

In the postwar years, Gund set a course for product and business expansion. Many new designs and themes were introduced for seasonal business opportunities (left). These springtime characters complemented the company's already popular Easter bunny business (below).

"We're Not Sticking Out **Our** Necks" . . .

We're giving you the straight facts when we say that, as blue-ribbon members of the "F. F. G." we carry forward a tradition of styling, quality and value that has been the heritage of all Gunds since 1898.

* * *

Be sure to see these GanderGunds and the other lovable characters in the Gund Easter line . . . on display in Gund showrooms from coast to coast. Plan your Easter buying soon because it's going to be an extra-early Easter in 1948.

*Famous Family of Gunds

Since 1898 **GUND** means real value in STUFFED TOYS

Gund NEW YORK • CHICAGO • SAN FRANCISCO • LOS ANGELES • SEATTLE **MANUFACTURING COMPANY**
J. SWEDLIN, INC., Successor, 200 Fifth Ave., New York, N. Y.

Quality has always distinguished Gund and its products. The hand-trimmed ponies seen to the right demonstrate the quality produced by the company. The animals pictured below all have the four-circle design, which was very popular for a decade. The name is derived from the circles of fabric ending each arm and leg. This design allowed Gund to choose a variety of fabrics and colors to trim each piece and complement the body fabric of the animal.

These unique designs show Gund's
ability to design highly stylized
products. All with textured plush
finishes, the dogs (left) were very
realistic representations for the day.
In addition, the rooster (below)
welcomes the new year.

Soft toys like these were the staple of Gund's line. It was common to use contrasting fabric on the center section of the toy's head and body (right). This added a colorful and bright splash to the product's appearance. Felt trimming on the rooster (below) allowed brightly colored trimmings to be added to the designs.

In 1947, L. John Swedlin succeeded Maxwell C. Sussman as the company's general sales manager, as seen to the left. John was assisted by Samuel Kaye; together, they successfully led Gund's sales team for more than 20 years. Leo A. Scherrer, a salesman in the Northwest, had three children—Donna, Spike, and Butch—who, as adults, continued to sell Gund products until the 1990s, a remarkable 60-year family tradition. The sales team of 1947 is named in the advertisement below.

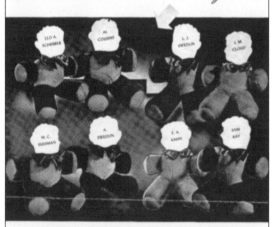

Gund announces its association with the Walt Disney Company, sealing a relationship that would last more than 60 years. Gund pioneered character licensing by creating plush toys from Disney's famous animated films and television programs.

A close association with Walt Disney Studios gave Gund Manufacturing Company the exclusive rights for the development of Mickey Mouse, Minnie Mouse, Donald Duck, Pluto and Winnie the Pooh. Gund later developed characters for King Features and Hanna Barbera.

© Walt Disney Productions

Gund's relationship with Disney flourished and its product line expanded, as the baby boom and growing postwar economy created many opportunities for established toy companies. An original Davy Crockett doll is featured in this advertisement.

In 1954 and 1955, Gund celebrated the opening of Disneyland in California with the introduction of many new plush items. Working closely with the Walt Disney Company, Gund maintained its market leadership by offering wonderful new soft toy products replicating those being shown on early children's television programming.

76

Gund pioneered the use of doll eyes, a vinyl face, and clothing on the soft plush toy. The unique and popular Bye-Bye Beagle, shown here, combined the company's Regal Beagle with a fun travel wardrobe.

Bye-Bye-Beagle is shown in its original condition. We are fortunate to have the toy in the company archives.

Gund Manufacturing Company
200 Fifth Avenue, New York City

EASTER ASSORTMENT No. 6900/3
Retail Price 69c

8929/3
Height 11½"
Colors—Pink
Blue & Sand

8939/3
Height 12"
Colors—Pink
Blue & Sand

8931/3
Height 8½"
Colors—Pink
Blue & Sand

328/3
Height 13"
Attractive Print Percale
Red
Felt Coat

329/3
Height 12"
Attractive Print Percale

330/3
Height 12"
Attractive Print Percale

PACKING TWO DOZEN TO THE BOX ASSORTED

These 1949 Easter bunnies sold in stores for 69¢! Each bunny had a percale outfit, balloon legs, four-circle hands and feet, and a rayon plush body.

Gund
Announces the Opening
of a New Showroom...

On or about February 8th 1952, the new Gund Showroom will be located in Suite 226, at 200 Fifth Avenue, New York City... These new quarters are just a few steps away from our previous sales office, but they represent an important step forward in our activities. It is fitting that we thank all those who, by their patronage, have made this possible.

Gund MANUFACTURING COMPANY
J. SWEDLIN, INC., *Successor*
200 Fifth Avenue, New York, N.Y.

In 1952, Gund expanded its New York City showrooms to include the adjacent Room 226. This space still serves as the main entrance to Gund's showroom during the toy industry's main event, Toy Fair, at the International Toy Center.

In its original condition, this Regal Beagle is a cherished possession on display at Gund headquarters in Edison, New Jersey.

Gund introduced its bestseller, Regal Beagle, in 1954. A highly styled dog with a vinyl face, it was the most popular toy Gund had created to date. Doll eyes were inserted into each vinyl head. These eyes opened and closed as the position of the dog changed. The face of each toy was painted by hand in the Brooklyn factory. Because of Regal Beagles's popularity, the company had to run a second shift of production. This soft and loveable toy squeaked as a child squeezed its snout.

In 1955, Gund produced toy dogs to launch the Disney film *Lady and the Tramp*. The Disney relationship proved very rewarding, as Gund repeatedly introduced new plush characters to coincide with the launch of feature films in theaters.

In the Gund archives, Lady and the Tramp appear as they originally did with the release of the feature film 50 years ago.

By 1963, the company's product lines had grown tremendously. Gund sold its own designs, and sales were supplemented with many licensed characters from the Hollywood studios, as seen in the advertisement to the right. The advertisement below lists the product lines offered by Gund at this time of great expansion and success.

The Disney line at Gund was extensive; original-condition samples of these toys were kept in the company archives. Shown below are molded, fabric-faced Mickey and Minnie, along with Donald and Pluto. The dressed Jiminy Cricket pictured to the left was made with a vinyl molded head.

Dumbo was a perfect Disney character to be produced by Gund. This original was produced with the launch of the movie in the mid-1940s.

Popeye and Sweet Pea were also produced by Gund in the postwar years. At that time, the company became the leader in the national soft toy industry, sustaining excellent relationships with all major Hollywood studios producing animation for children.

Young girls everywhere enjoyed one of Gund's best rag dolls of all time: Nancy Lou. This doll had a very soft body and a pressed-fabric face, which was produced on a mold and steam pressed into shape. Each face was hand painted, and the doll wore gingham dresses. These two photographs show the Nancy Lou dolls in Gund's archives.

This trade advertisement reports that the original Nancy Lou is available only from Gund. The company has always protected its original designs from infringement by other soft toy producers.

Products for girls have always been Gund's strongest pursuit, today as 50 years ago. Gund's bunnies and glamour stoles were created for the playful times of young ladies.

This Gund advertisement celebrates the polio vaccine and thanks Dr. Jonas Salk for making our world a happier, healthier place in which to live. Children's health has always been a subject of Gund philanthropy. At the time, the company celebrated this wonderful medical breakthrough.

In 1957, Gund moved to a brand-new manufacturing plant in Brooklyn. Affectionately known as Gunderland Park, the plant expanded its production to serve thousands of customers nationwide. From 1957 to 1974, the company produced its toys in this state-of-the-art, five-story factory and warehouse.

"Creative Center of the Stuffed Toy World" **Gunderland Park**

GUND HAS MOVED TO
A GREAT NEW PLANT

CROWNING EVENT IN GUND'S 59-YEAR HISTORY . . . This move to a new factory, the largest of its kind, is an important milestone in Gund's record of leadership . . . The entire Gund organization is proud of these new quarters . . . and looks ahead to even more noteworthy accomplishments at Gunderland Park. The great increases in space, equipment and facilities will enable us to produce more and happier Gunds than ever!

On this epic occasion, we extend sincere thanks to our patrons and friends whose encouragement and cooperation have been so vital to our steady progress.

The Swedlins

Gund Manufacturing Co.
J. Swedlin, Inc.

In the new Brooklyn factory showroom, Jack Swedlin (left), Herbert Raiffe (center), and his son Lance Raiffe discuss the Easter line of 1960. Lance, the eldest grandson of Jack, was interviewed for *Jack and Jill*, a children's magazine, in an article entitled "My Father Is a Toymaker."

Everyone Says the New Line is **Gunderful**

"High Spot of Gund's New Collection- Drawing Salvos of Applause!"

"New Pets of the Gund Family! Headliners of the Season!"

"Right in Tune with Demand! Right in Design! Right in Price!"

"Scoring a Smash Hit! Tops for Quality and Play Appeal!"

"Shopper-Stoppers All! Destined for Volume-Leadership!"

NEW STUFFED ANIMALS

creations by **Gund** "NEW FOR TOY FAIR"

New Different HAND PUPPETS by **Gund**

Going Great **Gund's** for 1957 OPEN AT TOY FAIR

Gund DESIGNS FOR 1957 NEW FOR TOY FAIR

NEW Unusual MUSICAL TOYS

NEW IRRESISTIBLE SOFT DOLLS NEW FOR TOY FAIR

IN STUFFED TOYS **Gund** means **Good**

You'll Be So Glad You Visited Room 226

© Walt Disney Productions

Gund Manufacturing Co. J. Swedlin, Inc. Room 226 200 Fifth Ave., New York 10, N.Y.

Visit Gund Showrooms at NEW YORK • CHICAGO • SAN FRANCISCO • LOS ANGELES • SEATTLE

For All Your Stuffed Toy Needs...All You need is **Gund**

NEW Walt Disney **Greats** NEW FOR TOY FAIR

TOP SECRET! New **Gund** Power Promotions for 1957

In 1957, the company boasted a wide variety of products for sale. With the postwar baby boom in full swing, Gund's market for children's products had never been stronger. The labels on the boxes in this advertisement reveal the many features offered and products produced in its new manufacturing facility.

Gund products from the 1935 line are shown in these early photographs. The dressed Felix the Cat toy was made by Gund to meet the release of this new character. Gund first produced Felix in 1921. With a cloth body and plush head, the toy had metal trimmings, leather holsters, and horsehair whiskers.

These puppets (above) were produced using the sketches shown on the facing page. Each character's head was sketched in several views and then formed in clay prior to the creation of the molds used in production. Each head produced was hand-painted prior to being attached to the fabric body. As an added feature, many of these puppets squeaked when the child's finger was inserted into the head. They were sold in a puppet show box for Disneyland guests (below).

DONALD DUCK
PUPPET HEAD DESIGN

MICKEY MOUSE
PUPPET HEAD DESIGN

PLUTO
PUPPET HEAD DESIGNS.

Most designs start with a sketch of some sort. These sketches show the vinyl heads that needed to be molded for the production of Disney character puppets. Sketches like these were likely submitted to Disney for approval prior to the sculpting of the heads and the casting of the molds.

In 1961, the Walt Disney Company received the rights to animate films and publish books using Winnie-the-Pooh. Gund was licensed the rights to produce this wonderful bear based upon the work of British author A. A. Milne and illustrator E. H. Shepard. Shown here is an original Gund Pooh bear from the year of his American debut.

Three
MODERNIZING A CENTURY-OLD TEDDY BUSINESS
1969–2004

These logos have represented the company and its products for the past 35 years. In 1970, Gund began using the logo with the bear head over the "U." However, in 1980, with the outset of its legendary consumer advertising campaign, Gund used "Gotta Getta Gund" almost exclusively. Many people actually believed the slogan "Gotta Getta Gund" was the company's name! This slogan has continued to appear on products for 24 years. BabyGund was introduced in 1990 and adorns all toys intended to be loved by infants.

In 1969, Herbert Raiffe became president of Gund upon the passing of John Swedlin. By that time, the company had become dependent upon licensed Disney characters such as Mickey Mouse for the majority of its business. This larger-than-life portrait of Mickey with a young girl exemplifies the significance of the Disney relationship to the company. Gund's dependence on licensed products was something Herbert Raiffe wanted to change. His vision has since enabled the company to rely on its own design team to support the majority of sales.

A 1969 press release contained this photograph of Herbert Raiffe, Gund's new president.

96

Through a set of unusual coincidences, a sound mechanism originally intended to be inserted into a stuffed clown became a bestseller itself. When the mechanism played its hearty laugh, everyone joined in. Placed in a fabric sack, as seen below, the product sold very well. The advertisement to the right features the Bag Full of Laughs and its successor, the Bag of Bull, which contained a mechanism that made a moo sound.

Through Herbert Raiffe's initiative, Gund expanded its product line into new and interesting stuffed toy animals. Pictured here is a Gund koala, a little-known bear to the national teddy market. The headline of "Happiness" in this 1970 promotion reflects the emotion Gund continues to bring its customers.

In 1972, Pres. Richard Nixon's historic trip to China to establish business and cultural relations resulted in a new Gund success story. As a gesture of friendship, the Chinese government gave the United States two panda bears who settled in the National Zoo in Washington, D.C. Gund immediately saw an opportunity to increase its business with stuffed panda bears. Herbert Raiffe was credited in *Forbes* magazine and other newspaper journals for his wisdom and foresight in marketing these products (right). UPI news service circulated this photograph and story, giving Gund national press coverage for its panda bears (below). Panda-monium ensued!

Plenty to go around

There'll be plenty of little Pandas around soon, thanks to the Gund Mfg. Co. of Brooklyn, which has speeded up its production of the stuffed animals since President Nixon's recent visit to Peking. A worker at the company examines one of the pandas. Herbert Raiffe, president of the company, acting on a hunch, decided last summer to step up the production of the pandas. (UPI)

Desmond and Rhoda were two "hip" rag dolls marketed by Gund in the early 1970s. The truth, not realized at the time, was that the hip kids did not want to play with rag dolls at all. These products, however, were representative of the company's ability to meet trends arising within the country.

In the early 1970s, hot colors and wild exaggerations of shape were popular features of stuffed animals. These early Gund beanies were colorful and floppy toys successfully sold as Plop-Pets.

Love. What a theme for a plush toy company selling Valentine's Day products! Toys from Valentine's Day 1971 are shown here in a company advertisement. Made of velveteen, these were some of Gund's earliest products imported from Japanese suppliers.

These leatherlike poodles were trimmed with real fur, creating a very posh 1970s appearance. The long eyelashes finished the look. The toys came in black, red, and yellow.

Going GONK

By MILDRED WHITEAKER

England — which gave "beatle" a brand new definition — is about to launch another weird word into U.S. orbit.

It's Gonk.

So what's Gonk? It's like "gonesville." If it's the coolest, maddest, mostest there is — it's Gonk. It will charm your blues and listen to your gripes. It's "gunderful." Just ask your British cousins.

Gonk is the surname of a fat little six-member family of stuffed creatures who have taken England by storm and

MAC GONK

UPSIDE-DOWN GONK

who are set for an American invasion in mid-September.

Gonk, a tartan-clad Scotsman, who plays the bagpipes to other members of the clan, including the Upside Down Gonk, who—naturally—stands on his head. There's the Eskimo Gonk (he's cool), and the Kinkie (clown) Gonk, and finally the hep Gone Gonk, whose hair hangs over his eyes.

According to long-distance reports from Gonk-conscious New Yorkers, British teenagers and their younger brothers and sisters succumbed to the Gonks almost as readily as they did to rock 'n roll. The word quickly became a part of their language. "Being Gonk" is like being "the most," absolutely "with it." A "Gonk party" is one that's a smashing success.

A 22-year-old American businessman just out of the Army is in part responsible for bringing Gonks to the U.S. When Carl Schulman saw a Gonk at his date's home (a gift her parents had brought from England), he was instantly smitten with the goofy creature which he describes as "a cross between Humpty Dumpty and a Schmoo."

He also recognized a good thing when he saw it.

And he just happened to have an uncle associated with a toy factory. The uncle, it turned out, had met the Gonks. His factory, Gund Manufacturing Co., had already made arrangements to produce Gonk toys in America.

Carl Schulman also happened to have parents in the children's wear business. The Schulmans—you guessed it—

THEY'RE 'GUNDERFUL' — When Ellen Smith, left, and Teresa Thompson met three members of the British Gonk family, they, too, decided that Gonks are "gunderful." They toy people, who are making

England merry right now, are set for an American invasion in September. Pictured, left to right, are Fred, the "People's Gonk," the hep "Gone Gonk," and the "Upside Down Gonk" who "couldn't care

less." Gonks will also be used as appliques on jumpers and sweat shirts. Ellen and Teresa, both 11, will be sixth graders at Howard Elementary School. P.S. They're "Beatle" fans, too.—Staff Photo

ANIMATED APPLIQUES—Marching into fall fashion, the Gonk clan will turn up as appliques on sweat shirts and on bright felt shirts.

Originally created in England in 1964, Gonks were brought to the United States by Gund (left). These mod characters were "gonesville, the coolest, maddest, mostest there is." Press articles and photographs (above) covered Gund's launch of these very unusual characters, which were produced in fabrics of bright, psychedelic color.

Gunderful VINYL INFLATABLE GONKS CHARM AMERICA!

MEET THE GONKS . . . adorable people . . . that are captivating young Americans with a new philosophy of life. These three-dimensional Vinyl Inflatable GONK caricatures are for carrying around and will make the playroom pad a gayer, GONK-happy place. GONKS are 13" tall, made of colorful plastic and will be the most adored possession of small GONKS! GONKS are the most . . . they convey a mute message of love for everyone they meet, and inflatable GONKS are ready to move into the lives of little boys and girls—everywhere! Each with poly bag and full color descriptive header.

Get GONK, Get GONK-profits with GONK-Volume.

I'm Kookie-GONK the Clown GONK

I'm Fred-GONK the people's GONK

I'm Gone-GONK I am the hep GONK

I'm Eskimo-GONK the cool GONK

I'm Upside-down GONK I couldn't care less

I'm Mac-GONK the bag-pipe playing GONK

© GONKS Ltd.

Gunderful by FRED

GONK INFLATABLE VINYL TOY

GK-160 INFLATABLE GONK ASSORTMENT

PACKING: 1 Dozen - Weight 3¼ lbs.
MASTER PACKING: 12 Dozen - Weight 40 lbs.

national sales offices and showrooms:
200 FIFTH AVENUE • NEW YORK, N. Y. 10010 • room no. 226   Tel: 212 OR. 5-7750

Chicago:	Los Angeles:	San Francisco:	Seattle:
Gund Mfg. Co.	E. A. Kahn Co.	E. A. Kahn Co.	Leo Scherrer Co.
14-112 Merchandise Mart	712 S. Olive Street	1355 Market Street	2840 N.W. 93rd Street
Chicago, Illinois 60654	Los Angeles, Calif. 90014	San Francisco, Calif. 94103	Seattle, Wash. 98107
Tel: 312 664-1631	Tel: 408 622-8684	Tel: 415 863-1006	Tel: 206 784-2184

Gund Manufacturing Co.
J. Swedlin, Inc.

Gonks were also sold as inflatable vinyl toys. Many styles of Gonks were available, including those shown in this assortment of inflatable products.

In April 1972, Sears Roebuck and Company, Gund's largest customer, awarded its Symbol of Excellence to Herbert Raiffe. Bill Fiffer, the infant product buyer for Sears, presented the award. He said, "It is only given to 394 of Sears's 13,000 suppliers and it represents the high quality of Gund's merchandise and the excellence of the firm's performance in shipping goods on schedule." For more than a decade, Gund served the Sears children's department with Winnie-the-Pooh products. Gund received the Symbol of Excellence Award for 12 consecutive years, placing the company at the highest level of vendor performance as measured by Sears.

Gund celebrated its receipt of the Symbol of Excellence with a party for all employees. Of course, Winnie-the-Pooh was the company's host, as seen to the right. The photograph below shows the presentation of the award to Herbert Raiffe. From left to right are Bill Fiffer, John Southworth, Herbert Raiffe, and Ernst Kaufman. This achievement was recognition of the company's dedication to quality manufacturing and on-time delivery.

In the late 1970s, the company's product line was being transformed from the traditional look of these Buddy Bears to the new look of the Golly Bears (shown on the next page). Buddy Bears were made of the finest and softest brown fabric available. But this still could not compare to the exquisite look of the multicolored fibers used to knit the fabric of the Golly Bears. Even the contrasting styles of these advertisements are representative of this dramatic change. For several years, many Gund products were photographed in beautiful natural surroundings.

it's GUND® INC. again!

gund inc. • 200 fifth ave., ny • suite 226 • (212) 675-7750

Circle No. 3 on produ

These Golly Bears, named for the sales manager of the company, Phil Golle, were photographed the day after an ice storm by Leo Slaninko of Lion's Den Studio. Leo's wonderfully creative displays, advertisements, packaging, and photography helped Gund to distinguish its unique product to the trade and to consumers.

In 1991, Gund received the New Jersey Business and Industry Association Award of Excellence. Presenting the award to Herbert Raiffe is Bruce Coe, president of NJBIA. In his acceptance remarks, Herbert spoke of Gund's never-ending desire to serve its customers with integrity and to produce items of the highest quality. These were the founding values of Adolf Gund and continue to lead the company today.

In the late 1970s, Gund partnered with a Taiwanese toy supplier, the Union Toy Company. This company served Gund's desire to provide lower-cost novelty plush toys. Seated at the table (above) are Rita and Herbert Raiffe discussing design, cost, and production issues. Working at the other end of the table (below) are, from left to right, two production managers, Joseph Yu, Bruce Raiffe, Roy Hsu, and a product merchandiser.

Gund needed additional production for its growing Winnie-the-Pooh business with Sears. Herbert Raiffe and Luis Amory review production on the floor of Gund's factory in El Salvador in 1978. Amongst political unrest in this nation, Gund was able to produce quality Winnie-the-Pooh products.

These views show the sewing department (above) and finishing department (below) of Gund's factory in San Salvador, El Salvador. The factory closed in 1982 due to political unrest in the country. Gund still employs Miriam Segura, an original employee of Gund's El Salvador facility.

Ain't Love GUND.

Gotta Getta GUND®

In 1980, Gund launched the "Gotta Getta Gund" magazine campaign. It featured photographs of Gund's most beautiful products with humorous "Gund-Puns" for headlines. This campaign firmly established the company's name as a well-known brand in the United States, Canada, England, and Australia. Even now, the company relies upon the "Gotta Getta Gund" slogan, as it represents the quality reputation Gund has earned. Shown in this advertisement, the Gund Snuffles bear is the best-known bear Gund has ever created.

Honey Bear (right) and Piggaletto (below) represent the cuteness and softness that have made Gund famous.

We've only just beGund.

Gotta Getta GUND®

Their name is Honey Bear.

Oink if you love Gund.

Gotta Getta GUND®

© 1985 Gund, Inc.

This little piggie is Piggaletto.
And you can getta Gund at all fine department, toy, gift and infants' stores.

The year 1983 marked the company's 85th anniversary and the launch of its collectible Gundy bear. The first bear on the left was unboxed, but all subsequent bears were boxed. This photograph shows the Gundy bears produced from 1983 to 1988. The Gundy bear has been produced as a limited edition each year through 2004. The tradition continues.

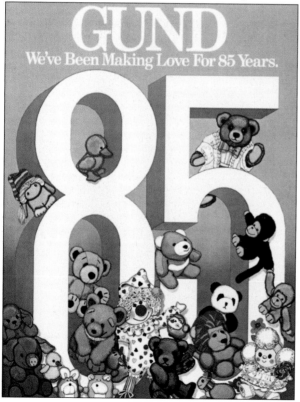

This poster captures the fun spirit enjoyed by the company as it celebrated its 85th anniversary of business. Pictured are some of the soft and huggable products Gund sold that year.

In February 1988, Gund celebrated its 90th anniversary with a party in the International Toy Center for its trade customers at Toy Fair. This photograph of the Last Elegant Bear and the Bialosky Bear was taken in front of the entrance to the celebration. From left to right are Bruce, Rita, and Herbert Raiffe.

For 10 years, George Knox Spangler led the Gund sales team to success. A retired lieutenant colonel of the U.S. Air Force, George commanded the sales team. Every sales meeting included memorizing drills of the product line and preparing for the many customers expected at trade fairs. George retired in 1990 and is still fondly remembered by associates and customers.

In her capacity as director of design, Rita Raiffe is credited for putting the "soft" in soft toys. Her insistence on huggable designs led the company to reduce stuffing and use softer textiles and gentler pattern making. This advertisement features Rita Raiffe and her collectible series of bears called the Signature Collection. Each bear was signed by Rita and sold in limited numbers (fewer than 1,000 pieces).

The Signature Collection, Gund's premier line of collectible bears, is a group of superbly crafted bears that have won prestigious awards. Pictured are just two of the dozen award-winning designs that have made Rita Raiffe's work famous. The Golden Teddy Award was given to Annie Arctic (left), a limited edition of 600 retired in 1993, and the TOBY (Teddy Bear of the Year) Award was given to Threadbear in 1993. He was an edition of 650 pieces. These annual awards are determined by a vote of collectors and shopkeepers.

Rita Raiffe created this standing Pooh bear for the teddy bear auction held in December 1994 at Epcot Center during its annual Teddy Bear Collectors Convention. It sold for $12,500. Truly a one-of-a-kind Gund Pooh, the fully jointed mohair bear wore a hand-knit cashmere sweater and carried a leather-bound book. It stood more than 30 inches tall and was sold with the stump from the Hundred Acre Wood.

Muttsy has been one of Gund's most successful dogs of all time. Here he is used to express a warning to competitors (left). Gund protects its designs with federal copyright registrations. With the help of its attorneys Marc Misthal (below, left) George Gottlieb (below, right), the company has successfully defended its designs in federal court dozens of times. Thanks to their wonderful legal counsel, Gund now enjoys a reputation amongst its competitors as a design innovator and a protector of its intellectual property.

Wide Wild World of Gund.

During the 1980s, Gund successfully sold soft toys using newly created textiles originally intended for the garment industry. The fabrics of the day were made of Japanese fibers using mod-acrylics to enable the textiles to be knit in new multicolors with extremely soft finishes. The resulting top-of-the-line products, like those pictured, defined Gund's position in the market as a producer of quality.

Celebrating Gund's 100th anniversary in 1998 required many special events. The parties included associates, customers, consumers, and several children's charities. In the photograph below, Rita Raiffe stands next to a portrait of her father and uncles working at Gund decades earlier. Above, Rita hugs the Gund anniversary bear auctioned in New York City, the proceeds of which were donated to children's charities.

Herbert Raiffe (right) and Bruce Raiffe (below) speak at Gund's formal anniversary celebration. The company enjoyed a huge turnout commemorating its wonderful success and congratulating the generations of associates who have helped Gund earn its stellar reputation.

Herbert (left), Rita, and Bruce Raiffe review the window display of Gund products in the FAO Schwarz store on Fifth Avenue in New York City. That same day, the 100th anniversary of Gund was discussed at a press event.

FAO Schwarz celebrated Gund's 100th anniversary by featuring 50-foot-high photographs of Snuffles and Muttsy in its Fifth Avenue windows. The store has been a Gund customer for more than 80 years.

Yoshi Sekiguchi of Tokyo, Japan, was the successful bidder, winning the Gund 100th-anniversary bear for a record $100,000. Gund contributed all of the proceeds to four children's charities, including the Pediatric AIDS Foundation and the Cerebral Palsy Association of Middlesex County. Mr. Sekiguchi returned to Japan with the bear, who now lives in a teddy museum and is visited by 50,000 people each year.

Celebrating Gund's anniversary are celebrity fans Mary Steenbergen and Dr. Ruth Westheimer. Standing with them is Dominick Ursino, president of the Cerebral Palsy Association of Middlesex County, a recipient of Gund's contribution from the $100,000 sale of its anniversary bear.

Special bear gets charities $100,000

By MARCOS PAGAN
STAFF WRITER

A buyer got more than a comfort toy for a successful bid of $100,000: a one-of-a-kind Gund teddy bear and donation of the proceeds to charity.

Proceeds from the auction yesterday at the William Doyle Galleries in New York City were donated to the Children's Hospital at Robert Wood Johnson University Hospital and the Cerebral Palsy Association of Middlesex County and two other national charities.

The bear was created to celebrate the 100th anniversary of Edison-based Gund, and the auction drew bidders from around the world. The winning bid came from Yoshihiro Sekiguchi, founder of two Teddy Bear Museums in Japan, who will feature the Centennial Bear in a third museum to open in Japan in August 1999.

"This bear is unique," said Gund President Bruce Raiffe. "We think it appropriate, in our 100th year, to auction this bear for more than $100,000. We think it even more appropriate, after a century dedicated to children, to distribute that money to charities that will benefit them."

The Centennial Bear was designed by Rita Swedlin Raiffe, an owner of Gund and its director of design, and presented in a handmade Plexiglas case with engraved brass name plate. It is made of a German mohair fabric colored in a new process the company will not repeat. A statement from Gund described it as a gradation of mocha brown at the base and warm mahogany at the tips.

Gund said the bear, fully jointed in the head, arms and legs, was made by one person under the direction of the designer.

Successful in its business endeavors, Gund has always striven to help the community. The Gund Foundation logo (left) was created with that purpose in mind. Each year, the foundation makes contributions of thousands of Gund toys to children in need. In the company's 100th-anniversary year, it contributed $100,000 amongst four children's charities (above).

The Gund Foundation was formed 20 years ago to provide children in "distressed situations" with a toy to hug. Since then, the foundation has contributed more than 500,000 Gund toys to sick, impoverished, or displaced children. Here, Herbert and Rita Raiffe attend an event hosted by Matilda Cuomo (center) in New York to support children in need.

Edison welcomes 10 cops

Toy maker buys vests for them

By JOSEPH PICARD
STAFF WRITER

The township police force has 10 new officers, several of whom received awards at yesterday's graduation at the Trenton Police Academy.

EDISON After the morning ceremony in Trenton, each of the graduates received a bulletproof vest, donated by Gund Inc., a toy manufacturer on Talmadge Road.

The new officers are Brett Bekiarian, Michael Carter, Salvatore Della Fave, Robert Dipple, Robert Dudash, Brian Favretto, Jason Gerba, Jonathan Kole, David Salardino and Thomas Wall. Each completed the 20-week course; their grades ranged from 91 to 96.

Della Fave, Dipple, Dudash and

Working closely with the Edison, New Jersey, police department has always been important to Gund. In this photograph, Mayor Spadoro (far left) and Bret Bekiarian (second from left) stand with Bruce Raiffe and Deputy Chief Bekiarian, who accepts 10 new bulletproof vests for the police officers. Gund has contributed many vests for the town's officers and has supplied funding for the new mounted police units.

125

At an annual company meeting, Bruce Raiffe (far left) presents five associates with diamond-studded Gund pins to celebrate their 20-plus-year association with the company. Gund is very fortunate to have loyal and hardworking associates, from left to right, Marie Hartman, Miriam Segura, Ken Taylor, Shelia Martinez, and Stacey Coleman.

In 1991, Doug Branch joined the company's sales division. Now serving as Gund's senior vice president of sales, special markets, he works closely with a design team and his customers to create unique Gund products that are exclusively produced for customers worldwide. These are only a few examples of the products and customers that have chosen to do business with Gund for their custom-item programs.

Celebrating the 100th anniversary of the naming of the teddy bear, the U.S. Postal Service chose to use a Gund bear on its commemorative stamp. Bruce Raiffe, accepting this honor on behalf of the company, spoke to more than 500 philatelic collectors attending the first day of issue ceremonies in Atlantic City, New Jersey. The stamp recognized both the 1902 naming of the teddy and Gund's founding four years earlier, in 1898.

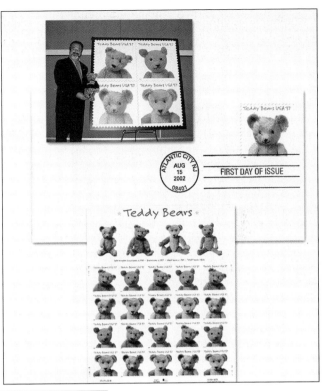

A worldwide operation, Gund is currently headquartered in Edison, New Jersey, but has a subsidiary in Preston, England, and offices in Hong Kong, China; Qingdao, China; and Seoul, Korea. In 1986, the company moved into its current world headquarters building in Edison, New Jersey. This 175,000-square-foot facility is home to the design center, executive, sales, and financial offices and is the East Coast distribution center for Gund's U.S. customers.

In July 2004, Bruce Raiffe became chairman and CEO, and Jim Madonna was promoted to president of Gund. Jim's appointment marks the first time that a non-founding family member has been given control of the company. With his many years of industry experience and a successful eight years at Gund, Jim offers Gund a unique opportunity for continued growth.

Eric Lohwasser (right) was promoted to executive vice president and CFO, and Ed Hayes (center) was promoted to executive vice president and COO in 2004. Their experience with the company and with the industry complement the team as Gund continues to grow. Jim, Eric, and Ed accepted their promotions with enthusiasm and excitement. Gund employs a wonderful leadership team and expects to build upon its history for many years to come.